# Magic Johnson

CHERRY LAKE PRESS

Published in the United States of America by Cherry Lake Publishing Group
Ann Arbor, Michigan
www.cherrylakepublishing.com

Reading Adviser: Beth Walker Gambro, MS, Ed., Reading Consultant, Yorkville, IL
Book Designer: Jennifer Wahi
Illustrator: Jeff Bane

Photo Credits: © Dmitrijs Kaminskis/Shutterstock, 5; © Sirisak_baokaew/Shutterstock, 7; © Dani Llao Calvet/Shutterstock, 9; © Sports Images/Dreamstime, 11; © EQRoy/Shutterstock, 13; © Jerry Coli/Dreamstime, 15, 17, 22; © Randy Miramontez/Shutterstock, 19, 23; © lev radin/Shutterstock, 21; Cover, 1, 8, 12, 16, Jeff Bane; Various frames throughout, Shutterstock

Library of Congress Cataloging-in-Publication Data

Names: Sarantou, Katlin, author. | Bane, Jeff, 1957- illustrator.
Title: Magic Johnson / Katlin Sarantou ; illustrated by Jeff Bane.
Description: Ann Arbor, Michigan : Cherry Lake Publishing, 2021. | Series: My itty-bitty bio | Includes index.
Identifiers: LCCN 2021008002 (print) | LCCN 2021008003 (ebook) | ISBN 9781534186897 (hardcover) | ISBN 9781534188297 (paperback) | ISBN 9781534189690 (pdf) | ISBN 9781534191099 (ebook)
Subjects: LCSH: Johnson, Earvin, 1959---Juvenile literature. | Basketball players--United States--Biography--Juvenile literature. | African American basketball players--Biography--Juvenile literature.
Classification: LCC GV884.J63 S26 2021  (print) | LCC GV884.J63  (ebook) | DDC 796.323/092 [B]--dc23
LC record available at https://lccn.loc.gov/2021008002
LC ebook record available at https://lccn.loc.gov/2021008003

Printed in the United States of America
Corporate Graphics

**About the author:** Katlin Sarantou grew up in the cornfields of Ohio. She enjoys reading and dreaming of faraway places.

**About the illustrator:** Jeff Bane and his two business partners own a studio along the American River in Folsom, California, home of the 1849 Gold Rush. When Jeff's not sketching or illustrating for clients, he's either swimming or kayaking in the river to relax.

My name is Earvin Johnson Jr.
But most people call me Magic.
I was born in 1959 in Michigan.

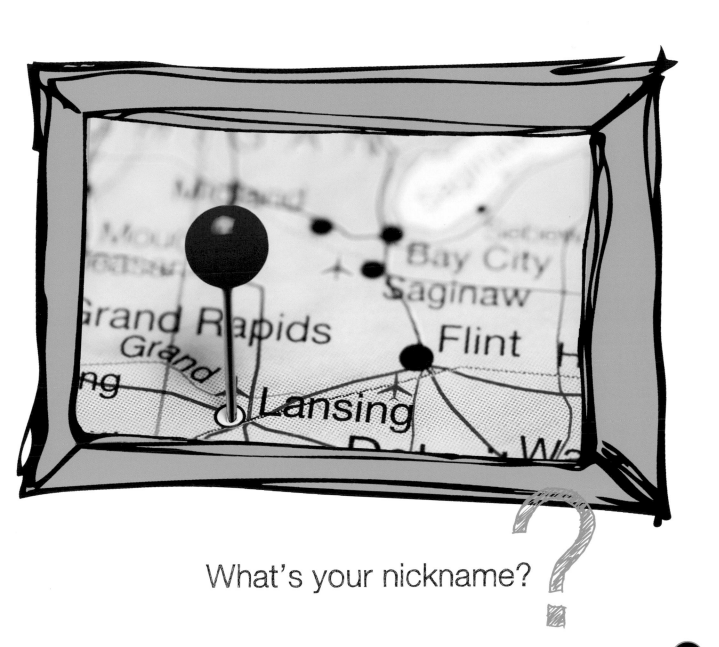

What's your nickname?

My parents worked really hard. They inspired me.

I helped my dad on his garbage routes. Other kids used to **tease** me.

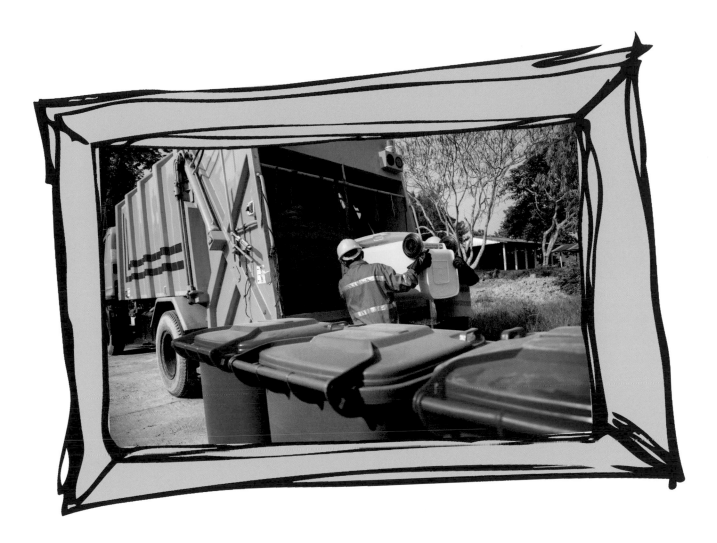

I loved playing basketball from a young age.

I was voted the best high school player in Michigan. **Colleges** noticed me.

I played for Michigan State University. We won the **NCAA** tournament. I was voted the Most **Outstanding** Player.

I was picked to play on a professional team. This was in 1979. I played with the Los Angeles Lakers in California. I got to play with Kareem Abdul-Jabbar.

Who is your favorite
basketball player?

I won many **championships**. In 1992, I played in the **Olympics**. We were called the "Dream Team." We won a gold medal.

I was named one of the 50 greatest players in **NBA** history.

I was added to the Basketball Hall of Fame. This happened in 2002.

I am **retired**. I use my time to help people understand **HIV**. I like teaching and giving back to people.

What would you like to ask me?

1992

1950

Born
1959

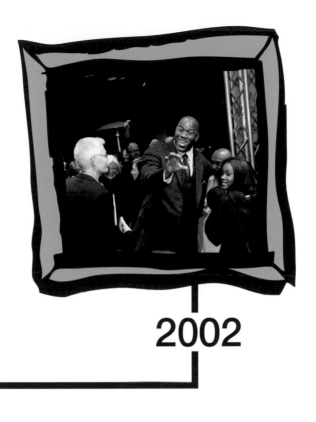

**2002**

**2060**

## glossary

**championships** (CHAM-pee-uhn-ships) final games in a sports series

**colleges** (KOL-ij-is) schools for higher education

**HIV** (AYCH EYE VEE) human immunodeficiency virus, which can lead to AIDS

**NBA** (EN BEE AY) the National Basketball Association

**NCAA** (EN CEE AY AY) the National Collegiate Athletic Association

**Olympics** (oh-LIM-piks) an international sporting event

**outstanding** (out-STAND-ing) very good

**retired** (ri-TIRED) left a job

**tease** (TEEZ) make fun of

## index